10 ⁰⁰

HANDBOOK FOR SPIRITUAL DIRECTEES
A Book of Spiritual Exercises

by

Philip St. Romain, M.S., D. Min.

- all rights reserved -

Lulu Press, 2010

ISBN: 978-0-557-77622-1

Also available as an eBook from the Apple iBookstore and Amazon.com Kindle Store.

Other works by Philip St. Romain can be found at:
http://shalomplace.com/psrbks.html

Dove artwork on cover was designed by Chris Sharp for an earlier work, *Handbook for Spiritual Growth*, by Liguori Publ.

Contents

Preface

Gathered together in this short volume are spiritual exercises that I have found helpful in my own life and in working with spiritual directees through the years. Most are from the Christian spiritual tradition, as that is what I am most familiar with. It would be fairly easy to adapt them to other religious traditions, however, and I leave that to the creativity of spiritual directors and directees to work out.

Although a spiritual direction session is generally open-ended and without a set agenda, it can be helpful at times to work through structured exercises such as those included in this book. The first few sessions, in particular, can include time to review what spiritual direction is about, how to prepare for a session, methods of prayer, and faith history. I have included these at the beginning of the book. Other exercises can be used as the director and directee see fit. Eventually, the Mission Statement and Rule of Life exercises can pull together and focus learnings and giftings of the Spirit.

Of course, people who are not in spiritual direction can benefit from practicing spiritual exercises as well. The title of this work, *Handbook for Spiritual Directees*, is not intended to imply that those who are not in spiritual direction would find this book irrelevant: hence, the subtitle.

I take little credit for the exercises presented herein. Most of them are a re-presentation or synthesis of material I have read or otherwise been exposed to through the years. Credit is given where my dependence on specific sources is obvious; sometimes this is not so easy to do, however.

May you enjoy this work as much as I have enjoyed compiling it.

Philip St. Romain

1.
What is Spiritual Direction?

(To be read and discussed by director and directee in the first or second session of spiritual direction.)

It is helpful to have a companion with whom you can share your joys and struggles in living the Christian life. This companion may be your spouse, another family member, or a close friend.

When we speak of spiritual direction, however, we are referring to a relationship that is more specifically focused on helping you to grow spiritually. A spiritual director listens and gives feedback about what he or she is hearing and sensing about the movement of the Holy Spirit in your life. This feedback is for your consideration only; the spiritual director is not a guru who tells you what to do.

The ideal of spiritual direction is soundly rooted in our understanding of Christian community. The Christian journey is not meant to be an individualistic, privatized spirituality. It is in community that we discover who we are and what we have to share. Spiritual direction provides an opportunity for a friendly and discerning experience of Christian community. As a community of two, you and your spiritual director attempt to discern what the Spirit is doing in your life and how you are being called to share your giftedness.

Spiritual Direction and Psychotherapy

From the foregoing, it should already be obvious that spiritual direction is fundamentally different from psychotherapy. A counselor is not concerned with your religious commitments nor with how the Holy Spirit is leading you. The goals of psychotherapy are different:

they are usually to help you deal with painful emotions and to support you in making difficult choices about relationships.

A spiritual director may deal with the same issues but from a quite different perspective. Painful feelings may be discussed in terms of how they lead away from God or toward God. Difficult relationships are also reviewed to discern how God is calling us to love other people and ourselves as well.

Because spiritual direction and psychotherapy have different goals and emphases, it is possible to benefit from both at the same time. A person who is in counseling should not refrain from spiritual direction because of it. Nor should anyone choose a spiritual director over a counselor. In fact, spiritual directors who guide people away from psychotherapy are doing their directees a disservice.

It sometimes happens that a spiritual director is also a trained counselor. Even so, the director and directee need to be clear about precisely what is going on in their work together.

Finally, we note that psychotherapists generally meet with their clients once a week or more. Such frequent meetings are necessary to process the many feelings and attitudinal changes going on in the person's life. Spiritual directors, on the other hand, seldom meet with directees more than once every two weeks in the beginning of the relationship. After a while, once a month is usually sufficient.

The Agenda in Spiritual Direction

Some spiritual directors have a set agenda for time spent with their directees; most do not. You will usually be allowed to talk about anything you have on your mind. If your sharing seems to have nothing to do with living the Christian life, the director will eventually try to steer the discussion in that direction by asking how what you have shared is affecting your prayer life or your relationship with God.

Usually, the first few meetings will be spent in becoming acquainted. The director will want to know all about your life. Telling your story to another in this way will help you come to know yourself better. The listening presence of the director is also a source of great healing. Because the spiritual director is not in the same role as a counselor, he or she may also choose, at times, to share about his or her life and faith journey, especially in the context of giving you feedback about something of relevance to your life. This can help you see the director as a fellow pilgrim on the journey rather than as a guru with all the answers.

After getting to know each other, you and the director may decide on a few structured activities to work on, or you may agree to go through a book on spiritual growth together. Many directors are trained in the Spiritual Exercises of Saint Ignatius and use these in some manner with their directees. Others know a great deal about keeping a personal journal and may encourage you to keep one if you haven't already started doing so. Most directors these days also respect the fact that different human temperaments are drawn in different ways by the Spirit, so they might want to help you discover your personality type.

As you can see, many kinds of issues can be discussed in spiritual direction. Of paramount importance, however, is your life of prayer. A spiritual director is one who will hold you accountable for daily prayer. He or she will be interested in hearing what is happening during your prayer and what you notice happening in your life as a consequence of prayer.

Choosing a Spiritual Director

We have already noted that a spiritual director is not a guru who will tell you what to do and what not to do. I would also like to make a distinction between a spiritual director and a sponsor in a Twelve Step program. A sponsor is one who has been in such a program for some time and can help new people learn how to recover from addictive involvements by using the Twelve Steps. This is a form of spiritual companionship, to be sure, but I recommend that your spiritual director be more than just a "big buddy" for the spiritual journey.

Ideally, your spiritual director should be a person with some formal training or experience in this area. He or she should have knowledge of the Christian spiritual tradition and should be at least generally familiar with psychological development. Your director should be a person of prayer who has attended one or more extended silent retreats. Finally, he or she should also be in spiritual direction with another and should have already worked through painful issues from the past.

I consider these minimal requirements for a Christian spiritual director. Generally, the ministry staff at a retreat center are good resources for finding a spiritual director. Most religious communities also have a few qualified people. Pastors can be found who meet these minimal requirements, and more lay people than ever are functioning effectively in this role.

If you do not already have a spiritual director and don't know whom to ask, I suggest you call your local retreat house. If you know of no such center, ask your pastor for advice, or visit the Spiritual Directors International web site (www.sdiworld.org) and their "Find a Spiritual Director" search tool, which lists spiritual directors who are members of the organization. Even after choosing someone, do not think you have to stay with that person. Agree with your director to give the relationship a trial for a while. Then, after a few sessions, evaluate whether you feel comfortable enough with each other to continue.

Fees for Spiritual Direction

It is typical for Christians to view ministry as something they have already paid for in the Sunday collection. This holds true for many local congregational or diocesan ministries, but not usually for spiritual direction.

Spiritual direction is really a professional service; therefore, be prepared to offer compensation to your director—especially if he or she is not an employee of an institution to which you contribute financially. Most (but not all) spiritual directors have a recommended fee for services, but would be willing to work something out if you cannot afford the full payment (do not count on health insurance to cover anything). As Jesus noted, "the laborer is worth payment" (Lk. 10:7).

Reflection

1. Why did you decide to seek spiritual direction?
2. What do you hope will happen to you through the process of spiritual direction?
3. What misgivings do you have about entering into spiritual direction?
4. What would you like to know more about concerning spiritual direction? Be sure to bring this to the attention of your director in your next session.

An earlier version of this chapter was originally published in *Handbook for Spiritual Growth,* by Philip St. Romain. Liguori Publications. 1994.

2.

Preparing for Spiritual Direction

Most spiritual directors have no objection to their directee talking about anything s/he feels is important at this time in life, even if they don't seem to have an explicit religious or spiritual focus. Knowing the overall context of the directee's life is important to your spiritual director. Also, most spiritual directors expect you to take some ownership for what you would like to discuss during a session.

Preparation can be very helpful for making the most of your time in spiritual direction. The following questions can help you to do so. You might consider journaling responses to them, or just reviewing them in advance.

1. What has been the general spiritual "tone" of your life lately? You might express this in terms of colors, temperature, aromas— anything that helps you to articulate your experience.
2. What events, experiences, relationships, etc. have communicated to you a sense of God's presence?
3. What events, experiences, relationships, etc. have communicated to you a sense of God's absence? Consider the role of attachments and addictions, here.
4. Describe your manner of prayer lately. How well does your prayer help you to experience conscious contact with God?
5. What kinds of decisions in your life have you searching for a sense of God's will?
6. In what area of life do you sense God calling you to growth? What lessons, values, disciplines, etc. are you being challenged to grow into? What can you do to honor this?
7. What kind of feedback would you like at this time from your spiritual director?

8. Anything else you want to talk about? (Open forum. Consider using some of the resources in this handbook.)

3.

Methods of Prayer

It is essential for anyone in spiritual direction (or interested in spiritual growth, for that matter) to have a regular practice of prayer. Discussing how things are going in prayer is one of the most important topics in spiritual direction.

First, let us acknowledge a distinction between prayer and prayerfulness. Prayerfulness refers to an attitude of openness to God's presence and guidance. We can be prayerful in this sense without actively saying or thinking prayers. It is doubtful that one can be prayerful without taking times for formal prayer, however. Indeed, one of the fruits of regular prayer is that it enables the deepening of prayerfulness.

Here, then, are a few basic notes and teachings about prayer from the Christian spiritual tradition.

Ingredients for Personal Prayer
(from *Becoming a New Person: Twelve Steps to Spiritual Growth*, by Philip St. Romain)

1. *Solitude:* "Whenever you pray, go to your room, close your door, and pray to your Father in private," commanded Jesus in Matthew 6:6. There is indeed much to be said for communal prayer, but private prayer cannot be replaced by any other activity. We must go some place where we can be alone and undisturbed; being alone with God is what is meant by solitude in prayer.

2. *Silence:* "In your prayers do not rattle on like the pagans. They think they will win a hearing by the sheer multiplication of words" (Matthew 6:7). Prayer time should be quiet time. Any

words and sentiments exchanged with God are done in the context of silence.

3. *Time:* Jesus spent entire nights in prayer; few of us can last fifteen minutes. Any time spent in prayer is probably better than no time at all, but it is doubtful that inner silence and a receptive listening to God's Word can take root in less than twenty minutes. Prayer time should also be prime time. Do not wait until you are tired and sleepy, for example, because it will be difficult to lift your mind and heart to God.

Vocal, Conversational Prayer

This is the form of prayer that comes most naturally, as it is simply addressing God either aloud or in one's thoughts in the same way we would address another person. You can do this at any time and in any circumstance. After doing so, listen to what God has to say in reply. Sometimes you can note a response in your thoughts, imagination or feeling; sometimes it is in the quality of silence that follows.

Praying With Scripture (Lectio Divina)

Lectio Divina (sacred reading) is an ancient way of praying with scripture or other texts. Practicing this form of prayer daily can help you to grow in your relationship with God. Journaling a few notes about your experience after a prayer session can also help to provide material to discuss in spiritual direction.

The approach to Lectio Divina I recommend is much less rigid than those you will find described in many places. In this approach, as in the classical one, we do identify the following movements:

1. *Lectio* – spiritual reading, preferably a passage of Scripture.

2. *Meditatio* – repeating the word or phrase that speaks to you; considering what it's saying to you if such reflections arise spontaneously.
3. *Oratio* – affective prayer; intercessions, gratitude, praise, just telling God where you are.
4. *Contemplatio* – simply resting in God in loving silence.

Many teachers have emphasized these movements, and have taught them as a four-step process, beginning with Lectio and proceeding in step-by-step fashion to Contemplation. That's too rigid and unnatural for many, however, so here's a more flexible format.

a. Set aside at least 20 minutes for the process. Pick out your passage. Be sure you're in a quiet place.
b. Begin with vocal prayer, dedicating your time to draw close to God. Invite the Holy Spirit to lead you in this prayer time.
c. Spend a few moments just quieting yourself, noting your breathing, the feel of your body, the sense of being where you are. Ask yourself which of the four movements you feel drawn to at this time – e.g., it's OK to begin by resting in God if such a grace is already given, or to voice prayers of petition or gratitude, etc. You might also just want to tell God "where you are."
d. When you feel ready to read the passage, do so, slowly, reverently. Let the words wash over you and sink in as they will. Take a couple minutes of silence afterward and then read the passage again, slowly, prayerfully. Silence. If distractions arise, just notice them and return to the practice.

e. If a particular word or phrase speaks to you, repeat it in your mind. Let its message really sink in until you no longer feel like repeating it. Silence.

f. Talk to God about how this word has spoken to you. What considerations . . . questions . . . feelings . . . concerns, etc.?

g. When you have expressed yourself to God, pause for a minute or two of silence. If you feel drawn to continue resting in silence, do so. If not, return to your passage and read from where you left off. If another word or phrase speaks to you, repeat Steps E and F.

h. Continue doing this until you feel you have completed your prayer time.

Contemplative Prayer Methods

In contemplative practice, we open ourselves to God beyond thoughts and words. As with Lectio Divina, it usually entails setting aside a period of at least 20 minutes for silence and solitude. What follows are four popular methods.

1. *Centering Prayer.* This popular practice can be used in the context of Lectio Divina, which is where it rightly belongs. It is really an adaptation of E in the practice described above, wherein one would simply repeat the particular word until it leads you to silence and resting in God, and continue to do so when distractions arise. For more information, go to http://www.centeringprayer.com/

2. *Christian Meditation.* Developed by John Main, this practice entails mentally repeating the word, *maranatha*, for 20 minutes. As such, it is a form of mantra meditation. You can find out more about this practice and its history by visiting the web url: http://www.christianmeditation11step.org/howtomeditate.html

3. *Hesychast Prayer (Quiet Prayer).* This form of contemplative practice was widely used by the fathers and mothers of the desert in the early days of Christianity. At least two 20 minute prayer periods are recommended. Practice of this prayer may lead to feelings of warmth in the heart and perception of inner light. Enjoy. . .

A. Sit quietly, with back straight and hands resting in the lap, palms up.

B. Lovingly introduce into your mind the prayer, "Lord Jesus Christ, Son of God, have mercy on me." (Note: this may be shortened as the prayer proceeds).

C. Let this prayer move in synchrony with your breath, praying the first part with your inhalation, the second with exhalation.

D. When distracting thoughts attempt to break in, persist with the Jesus Prayer. Allow yourself to feel your emotions, however.

4. *Breath Prayer.* Simply be attentive to your breathing. Do not try to breathe deeply or quickly; just normal breathing will do. Offer your breathing to God; invite the Holy Spirit to energize you with the Breath of God. When you notice your mind becoming interested in a distraction, simply return to your breathing.

One variation of this prayer is to use a prayer phrase in synchrony with your breathing, much as you would in Hesychast Prayer. You can use whatever word or phrase you wish as you inhale and another as you exhale. When your distractions cease, you can drop the word or phrase.

4.

Daily Review

Here is a practice used by many at the end of the day to see what lessons can be learned and how God was present and active through the day. Set aside fifteen to twenty minutes at the end of the day for prayer and review of your day. A suggested format is described below. Journaling your responses can also be helpful.

1. Take a few moments of quiet. Breathe deeply. Ask God to help you see yourself as you truly were during the day.
2. Look back over your day - not to see what you did wrong but to honestly acknowledge what was going on with you and others.
   * What happened? What did I do today?
   * How did I feel? Why did I feel that way?
   * Were my expectations and beliefs reasonable?
3. Affirm the healthy things you recognize.
4. Admit to yourself and God the unhealthy things. Ask God's forgiveness, believe it is yours, then decide if you need to apologize or make amends.
5. Use creative visualization to grow stronger. Honestly acknowledge the troubling situations of the day. See and feel yourself acting honestly and lovingly in these situations. Ask God for the grace to help you act in this new way.
6. Close with simple awareness of the sights and sounds around you, grateful for the good things in your life.

This process can be undertaken as a daily journal exercise or by prayerfully reviewing your day in your own mind. I like to take a walk before bedtime for examen. The important thing is to do it. It is a discipline, to be sure, but a very important one.

Philip St. Romain

Awareness Examen (Consciousness Examen)

Here is another way to look back on your day. It is similar to the Daily Review exercise we just discussed, only it is more attuned to how God was present and active in your day. You can do the exercise in your journal, or by just prayerfully glancing back on your day.

Begin by settling in. Spend a few moments getting comfortable. Relax. Try to clear your mind of distracting thoughts, but do not be disconcerted if you do not succeed at this completely.

Next, thank God for your day and for the graces you have been given. Ask the Holy Spirit to help you look back on your day and see your behaviors and motives as God saw them.

Once you are prayerfully present to God, review your day and note if you were aware of God's presence or just doing your own thing, without openness to God. Take your time in doing so and talk to God about this as you go through the events of the day. Ask forgiveness for times of self-centeredness, and give thanks for the graces given through the day.

The Awareness Examen is strongly emphasized in Jesuit spirituality. For a more fully developed discussion of this topic and how to practice the examen, see the web link below:
http://www.jesuits.ca/orientations/examen.htm

5.

Johari Window

This resource is often used as a tool for personal growth and to help facilitate better relationships. You can use it to help sort issues in your relationship with God. Consider the diagram below:

	Self	Others
Others	A. Open Self	B. Blind Self
Self	C. Secret Self	D. Hidden Self

    A. Open Self - what you and others know about you.
    B. Blind Self - what others see, but you do not.
    C. Secret Self - what you know, but others do not.
    D. Hidden Self - what neither you nor others know.

In your life with God . . .
1. What do you share with God about yourself? How do you feel yourself belonging to God, and God to you? What constitutes the Open part of your relationship?
2. What do you hide from God (even though God knows what that is)? What do you withhold? What belongs to the Secret part of your relationship?
3. What do you think God sees in you that you might not be aware of (Blind spot)? What do you hear from Scripture? Church teaching? What do you think your spiritual director might say, here?
4. How open are you to the Hidden aspects of your being?

6.
Faith History

This exercise can help you to reflect on your own spiritual development through the years. There are a number of ways to proceed. Some people like drawing a time line and jotting key words concerning what was happening through the years. Another more systematic approach is to make a table, with several headings, and notes in the table cells. Whatever approach you choose, here are some considerations to include.

A. *Time of life.*
   You can do this by year or, better, by periods that were fairly consistent. E.g., pre-school years, grade school, etc. You could also consider what places you lived, or such events as life before and after a divorce or job loss. These are, in other words, periods or seasons of your life, including the one you live in at this time. See if you can come up with a creative name for each of these times in your life.
B. *What was going on in each time of your life?*
   Where did you live? What were you doing? What was family life like? Who were your friends? Getting in touch with these specifics can help you to be more deeply in touch with what each time of life was like for you.
C. *What was faith like for you?*
   What did you believe about God in each time of life? What influenced your beliefs? Were there times of closeness to God? Doubts? Desolations? What religious or spiritual community did you belong to? What was that like?
This exercise can help you and your spiritual director become more aware of the "big picture" of how God has been working in your life.

7.
Examen of Relationships

This exercise is a good follow-up to the one on faith history, but can also be done at any time. Take your time and do not hurry through this exercise.

1. Looking back on the different times of your life, make a list of the people with whom you were engaged in important relationships. Include parents, siblings, teachers, relatives, friends, etc.
2. Pick one period and rank the relationships in order of importance to you.
3. Consider the gifts you received from each of these relationships. How was God's love manifest through this person? Let specific memories emerge. What lessons did you learn? Give thanks for these blessings.
4. What hurts and struggles did you experience from each of these relationships? Be specific. How have these influenced your growth and development? If you note lingering resentments, resolve to enter into a process of forgiveness that you might be more free within yourself.
5. After going through the relationships in one period of your life, move on to another period and repeat steps 2-4.

8.

Clarifying Your Images of God and Creation

How we understand God and creation is foundational to one's spiritual perspective. Discussing this topic in spiritual direction with the goal of clarifying your own viewpoint can be most helpful, from time to time.

What follows are a few ways of imaging and conceptualizing how God and creation interact and co-exist. See what you think . . . where your own beliefs lie. Ask your spiritual director to share his or her own perspective so the two of you will know where you're coming from on this issue.

How God and Creation Co-exist

A. *Monism / pantheism* - creation is really God manifesting *as* all these diverse forms. The universe is something akin to "God's body," with God's Being manifesting through all these forms. Ultimately, this view makes no essential distinctions between God and creation and tends to view God as primarily immanent, or within, creation.

B. *Deism* - God created the universe, then retired to the supernatural realm, allowing creation to work itself out according to the lawfulness instilled within it by God. Some call this image of God "The Divine Clock-maker," as God winds up the universe, then allows it to spin out without any interference or intercession by God. This view stresses learning about the lawfulness of the universe and adapting one's life to it. The God of this universe is entirely transcendent, or external to creation.

C. *Theistic revelation* - similar to deism, only God is more involved in shaping the universe through occasional periods of intervention and revelation. These revelations help to clarify and supplement our understanding of the moral and spiritual order of the universe that we might better direct our lives according to these norms.

D. *Panentheistic creationism* - God created the universe and sustains it in being; God dwells within creation and in a transcendent, supernatural realm as well (immanent and transcendent). Creatures depend upon God for their existence, and also possess their own intelligence and freedom, which they may use in conformity with God's ways, or in defiance thereof. God and creatures (especially spiritual beings) co-create through a shared medium of influence (thoughts, images, energies, love). God is both within and beyond the universe.

You will find these four views and various combinations of them in almost all the world religions. In general, it seems that most Eastern religions are A., Judaism and Islam are C., Christianity is D, while there are many instances of B. However, you can find examples of all four positions within most religions, though some will be considered more representative of a given religion than others. It should also be noted that within some of these positions, there is variation; e.g., some distinguish between different types of monism/pantheism.

God's Moral Character

Given the four perspectives above, there remain other considerations, this one pertaining to whether God is caring, disinterested, or antagonistic. These views can overlap with the above perspectives.

A. *Antagonistic attitude.* God is a "troubled Being" who basically projects and acts out on creation. Monists might consider the creation to be a way that God is trying to work out God's own "imbalances" or defects of character. Deists with this view of God would consider creation a "cruel joke." Other theist/panentheist positions would view creation as doomed to disorder and decay because it is ultimately derived from a malevolent Being. Needless to say, this view breeds cynicism and pessimism.

B. *Disinterested attitude.* God could care less how creation unfolds, as God has done all that is justly required in creating a lawful universe. If the universe fails, this is no reflection on God, who is already happy in heaven. Primarily a deist position, although it can creep into the mindset of other theists as well. This viewpoint leads to apathy.

C. *Loving attitude.* The universe is an expression of God's goodness and love and exists to share in God's happiness. All four perspectives can affirm this position, though each in its own way.

God's Gender

This consideration has less to do with God's interaction with creation, although in some systems of thought, it is very relevant. Which of the following viewpoints makes the most sense to you?

A. *God is primarily masculine.* Predominates where creating is considered a masculine characteristic and creation a feminine or receptive role.

B. *God is primarily feminine.* The feminine role is to give birth; the universe is "God's baby," as it were. God as nurturing, persevering, divine mother.

C. *God is equally masculine and feminine.* Both qualities exist in balanced measure in God.

D. *God is trans-gender.* Masculinity and femininity do not exist in God except, perhaps, analogously to our human understanding of the term. God has no gender, but can still be understood as personal—i.e, a Being who has intelligence and will/intentionality.

Further considerations

1. What kind of image of God emerges for you from these considerations?

2. How does this image relate to the teachings of your religious tradition?
3. How does this image influence your prayer? Your faith? Your lifestyle?
4. What other considerations or questions concerning your image of God do you still need to have clarified?

9.

Guidelines for Discernment

- from Pathways to Serenity, by Philip St. Romain -

Discernment, here, refers to getting a sense of what God's will might be in a given situation – especially one in which you must make a decision between two or more options. In Christian spirituality, it is based on the following assumptions:

- God is a good God, who wants to give you much more than you want for yourself.
- God knows who you are better than you know yourself. God also knows what you need in order to become the person God created you to be better than you know what you need for this.
- When you are faced with a number of options, it is entirely possible that some of these options are better for you in terms of your overall human objectives than others.
- When you surrender your preferences for different options to God, you become free to discern God's preference (if any) among these options.

Unless you accept these assumptions (at least on an intellectual level), the guidelines that follow will not make much sense.

The truly great master of the art of discernment was Saint Ignatius of Loyola. His writings on making choices and discerning God's call have stood the test of time and continue to provide a helpful structure for choosing among options. For this reason the guidelines presented here rely heavily upon the genius of Ignatius.

General Principles

1. When you are making a decision or choice, you are not deliberating about choices which involve sin [wrongdoing] but

rather you are considering alternatives which are lawful and good. . ." (Saint Ignatius)

2. It is not necessary to agonize over God's will in choosing between healthy options in the small affairs of everyday life."Ordinarily there is nothing of such obvious importance in one rather than the other that there is need to go into long deliberation over it. You must proceed in good faith and without making subtle distinctions in such affairs and, as Saint Basil says, do freely what seems good to you, so as not to weary your mind, waste your time, and put yourself in danger of disquiet, scruples, and superstition" (Saint Francis de Sales).

3. In areas where you have binding commitments (marriage vows, parenting, religious vows, and so forth), "your basic attitude should be that the only choice still called for is the full-hearted gift of self to this state of life" (Saint Ignatius). In other words, every effort must be made to live out the implications of your binding commitments, even if those commitments were made poorly.

4. In areas of life where you have already made decisions (which can be changed) on the basis of God's call, "your one desire should be to find your continued growth in the way of life you have chosen" (Saint Ignatius).

5. "If you have come to a poor decision in matters that are changeable, you should try to make a choice in the proper way whether it would be maintaining the same pattern of life or it would demand a change" (Saint Ignatius).

6. If possible, you should avoid making important life decisions during times when you are emotionally upset, for it is likely that you shall then be running away from a problem rather than responding to God's call.

7. When attempting to discern among a number of options regarding significant lifestyle choices, you should proceed as Saint Ignatius suggests below.

A. First Pattern for Reviewing Options
- Clearly place before your mind what it is you want to decide about. What are your options?
- Attempt to view each option with equal detachment, surrendering personal preferences to God.
- Sincerely pray that God will enlighten and draw you in the direction leading to his praise and glory.
- List and weigh the advantages and disadvantages of the various dimensions of your proposed decision.
- Consider now which alternative seems more reasonable. Then decide according to the more weighty motives and not from any selfish or sensual inclination."
- Having come to the decision, now turn to God again and ask him to accept and confirm it—if it is for his greater service and glory—by giving you a sense of serenity and holy conviction about this decision

B. Second Pattern for Reviewing Options: (This is an excellent follow-up on the First Pattern to "objectively" evaluate your decision.)
- Since the love of God should motivate your life, you should check yourself to see whether your attachment for the object of choice is solely because of your Creator and Lord.
- Imagine yourself in the presence of a person whom you have never met before, but who has sought your help in an attempt to respond better to God's call. Review what you would tell that person and then observe the advice which you would so readily give to another for whom you want the best.
- Ask yourself if at the moment of death you would make the same decision you are making now. Guide yourself by this insight and make your present decision in conformity with it.

- See yourself standing before Christ your Judge when this life has ended and talking with him about the decision which you have made at this moment in your life. Choose now the course of action which you feel will give you happiness and joy in the presence of Christ on the Day of Judgment.

There is a big difference between reacting to life and responding to God's call. In the small self, you spend much time reacting to life; you allow other people and circumstances to greatly influence your behavior. By undertaking a decision-making process such as that outlined above, you become more pro-active, or responsive to God's call. As with all the other spiritual living skills, right discernment will involve practice and checking matters out with the community. The fruit of this discernment will be fuller growth and deeper serenity — two very good reasons to persist in the struggle to discern God's call.

10.

The Nature of Attachments

- a few notes -

What are the obstacles to growth in your relationship with God? There are many levels of response to this question, but one way to approach it is to examine the topic of attachments. The definitions and notes below can help to stimulate your own thinking about how you experience disordered desires, attachments and addictions in your life.

Desire—the attraction of the will toward any particular person, place, or thing.

A. It is natural and inevitable for a created being with needs to have desires.

B. Our deepest, most fundamental desires are to live, to understand, and to be happy; these desires can ultimately be fulfilled only in God.

Disordered Desires—the inappropriate attraction of the will toward any particular person, place, or thing.

A. To have what you do not want (but what you cannot be rid of without violating your moral values).

B. To want what you do not have (in such a manner as to undermine your experience of what you need most . . . i.e. union with God).

- The fulfillment of such a desire hurts oneself or others.
- The pursuit of such a desire violates moral values.
- The cultivation of such a desire undermines the experience of God as the fulfillment of our deepest desire.

Attachments—disordered desires that have become more or less habitual preoccupations of the mind and will.

A. Examples: approval of others, winning, controlling other people and circumstances, accumulating money, sexual experience., getting high on something, perfect work, losing weight, etc.

B. Effects on consciousness:
- Intellect is preoccupied with ways to get what you want and avoid what you don't want; other people seen as a help or a hindrance to obtaining attachment.; judgmentalism.
- Will is focused on getting what I want . . . selfishness
- Emotional climate is disturbed. Anxiety about not getting what I want; angry toward threats to my fulfillment.
- Attention is focused on past and future. NOW is missed.
- Experience of God: One who can help me get what I want.

Addictions—attachments that have become compulsive preoccupations. The mind and will are no longer capable of completely resisting indulgence.

Spiritual Significance of Attachments/Addictions: They are our primary obstacle to experiencing peace. . . happiness . . . union with God.

How to Know if You Have Attachments

1. Do you experience anxiety over situations beyond your control?
2. Is your mind "noisy," preoccupied over concern about which you derive little pleasure in considering?
3. Is it difficult for you to enjoy the NOW without disturbing memories from the past or anxious concerns about the future intruding?

—If you answer yes to any of these questions, you have an unhealthy attachment of some kind. Now the task is to name them and begin to work with them, which will be the concern of our next exercise.

11.
How to Drop an Attachment/Addiction
- a few notes -

What follows are guidelines for identifying attachments and working to let them go. Sharing your experiences in doing so with your spiritual director is most appropriate, and can support your intent to be free from harmful attachments.

Symptoms of Attachment:
1. Anxious preoccupation: restless thinking, judgmentalism.
2. Lack of serenity.

Quick Way to Drop an Attachment
1. Notice anxious preoccupation and its major themes. Verbalize these to God.
2. If no immediate action is required, say the Serenity Prayer, asking God to care for specific things not in your control, and to give you the grace to trust in God's Providence in your life.
3. Bring your attention into the Now, and do what you're doing. The anxious preoccupation will fall away in short order if you do not indulge it behaviorally or mentally.

For Stubborn Attachments and Addictions
1. Notice preoccupation and its major themes. Write these down. Ex. "I feel anxious about (topic) because (consequences)."

2. Turn each theme into a question?
    "How can I be sure that. . ."
    "What to say to impress so and so?"
    "How to be sure I will have enough money?"
3. See how much this question has influenced your thinking and behavior. Make a list of past decisions and behavior related to this question. Ask God for the grace to be free of this disordered desire.
4. See how this behavior has affected you and others. Make a list.
5. Resolve to make amends where your behavior in reference to this issue has hurt another. Ask God for forgiveness. Sacrament of Reconciliation.
6. What real need (if any) is this question addressing?
7. What is the appropriate or prudent way to meet this need?
8. In your imagination, see yourself meeting this need appropriately. Ask for Divine Guidance to see how to do this, and to desire this kind of responsible behavior.
9. If old preoccupations arise, see and acknowledge them non-judgmentally, but do not indulge them. This is the true meaning of abstinence. Bring your attention into the Now, and do what you're doing. If it is time to meet your real need in the manner you decided on in #8, go ahead and do so in awareness and gratitude.

When All Else Fails

After doing the above for some time, it may become obvious that a compulsive attachment is so deeply rooted that you need additional help. Do not hesitate to ask for it. Help is available in the various Twelve Step groups and in addiction treatment programs.

12.

Origin of the False Self System

- a few notes -

The False Self System is not a real self, but a system of conditioning we develop from early childhood onward to compensate for non-loving influences in our lives. It is important to see how this works in one's consciousness, as False Self conditioning moves us to develop attachments and addictions.

After reading through the points in this reflection, discuss with your spiritual director how you relate to them in your own life. The attitudes listed in point #5 are especially important to consider.

---

1. *Perception of a conditionally loving developmental environment (begins in the womb).*
   a. Body-feeling perception. Feeling rejected or conditionally accepted and loved.
   b. Splitting of feeling self into natural/wounded elements. Experience of fear, shame, hurt, anger.

2. *Defensive contraction of psychic energy away from unconditional relationship with the environment by contracting the will.*
   a. Decreases vulnerability to environment.
   b. Provides sense of existence of psychic energy that "belongs to me," "is mine," within "walls" of contraction. Provides sense of a "me-they-can't touch, or hurt." Beginning of the delusion of non-relational autonomy, and the deepest level of the False Self system. Origin of relational alienation, willfulness, sin.

c. Diminishes experience of "natural" union with the Divine, Who is the true Source of all energy and existence.

3. *Internalization of unhealthy rules from the environment; development of a Critical Parent system of internal programming.*
   a. It's not OK to talk about problems.
   b. Feelings should not be expressed openly and directly.
   c. Communication is best if indirect, with one person acting as messenger between two others (triangulation).
   d. Unreasonable expectations: always be happy, be strong, be perfect, be in control of your feelings.
   e. You are responsible for how others feel ("make us proud").
   f. Don't be selfish (which includes even legitimate self-love).
   g. Do as I say, not as I do (unhealthy modeling).
   h. It's not OK to play or be playful.
   i. Don't rock the boat. Peace at any price.
      (from *Lost in the Shuffle,* by Robert Subby)

4. *Disempowerment of rational and volitional powers*
   a. Inner tensions between affective system and critical attitudes drains us of energy.
   b. Critical attitude from other people and toward oneself further reinforces commitment to look to others to decide for us the values by which we will live.

5. *Crystallization of the False Self Ego, or Survival System of Consciousness (occurs as early as five years of age).*
   a. I am conditionally lovable and acceptable.
   b. The conditions for getting love and acceptance are defined by Critical Parent. These conditions spell out the kinds of things I must do to be loved and accepted.

c.   Therefore, I will adopt a life stance that will allow me to maximize opportunities for approval, and minimize my experiences of disapproval.

d.   This life stance will have its center "outside of self," in other people ', activities, things, and in an utterly Transcendent, judgmental God.

e.   This life stance will assume a shape in the various roles I play. My giftedness will be expressed in the context of these roles.

f.   I will maintain myself in these roles by using addictive fixes. These fixes keep me out of touch with my inner emotional experiences, and keep my center "outside of self."

13.

Characteristics of the False Self System

Consider the characteristics of the false self system listed below. For each that applies to you, write out how you experience this in your everyday life, and what consequences you and others suffer because of this.

---

1. I am more in touch with what I want for my life than what God wants for my life.
2. I frequently feel numb, empty, or cranky inside myself.
3. I am afraid to discover what's really going on deep inside of myself, and so I try to avoid this by living on a more superficial level.
4. When I become uncomfortable inside myself, I find some way to escape from this discomfort by using television, food, work, a relationship, alcohol, drugs, shopping, gambling, reading material, religious activities, or chatter.
5. I am often critical of myself.
6. I am often critical of others.
7. My mind is often filled with anxious preoccupations about the future, and if I will be able to get or have what I think I need.
8. It is difficult for me to just *be*. I generally feel that I must be *doing something* to justify my life to myself and others.
9. I am trying to find happiness by getting something I don't have, or getting rid of something I do have but don't want.
10. In relationships with others, I generally feel like I have to play a role, or wear a mask. If I would not do this, the other would probably reject me.

11. Frequently, I do not even know what my true thoughts and feelings are.

12. My self-concept or idea of myself is skewed, so that I see myself as inferior to others, or I see myself as superior to others.

13. I am constantly comparing myself to others to determine if I am "ahead" of them or "behind" them in some area of life.

14. When people insult or ridicule something or someone I am identified with, I feel personally insulted and I become angry.
    - - E. g. When my country is put down, I become defensive.

15. The roles I play give me a sense of identity. What I do is who I am. If I could not do, I would not know who I am.

16. When someone criticizes the way I do something, I feel personally put down. I have a hard time separating what I do from my identity

17. It seems that all my thoughts, feelings, memories, and desires are related to my self-image—to changing it, or maintaining it.

18. If I could better control the people and external circumstances in my life, I would be happier.

19. I tend to view close friends and family members as "mine." I tend to treat them that way, too.

20. I tend to view God as judgmental. I believe I have to do the right things—usually religious kinds of behaviors—to win God's approval. I seldom feel that I am in harmony with God.

21. It is difficult for me to see how God is involved in the everyday affairs of my life. Generally. it seems that God has nothing to do with me and my life. God has better things to do.

22. In my prayer, I spend more time asking God to do what I want, than praying for the grace to do what God wants.

14.

A Short Summary of Spiritual Theology
- a few notes -

What follows is a general perspective on spiritual theology that can help to encourage deepening relationship with God. Consider these points and notice your inner response to them. Do you agree? Disagree? Why? Why not? Discuss with your spiritual director.

A. Just as the body is already in the soul and the soul in the body, so, too, God is already in the soul, and the soul in God.

B. God is always present to the soul, giving it life, loving it, attempting to lead it to become what God has created it to be.

C. Attachments and addictions create disturbances in the soul that prevent one from knowing God's presence and responding to the leadings of the Spirit.

D. Nevertheless, even in this state of disturbance, one can begin to relate to God in whatever way is most meaningful. Jesus Christ is God's invitation to a return to full union.

E. By loving God and others while dropping attachments and addictions, the False Self will be put to death and the True Self born. This is sometimes a painful process—a cross that heals the soul.

F. Through the dark nights of transformation, the soul is drawn into deeper and deeper realms of silence that transcend thought and feeling. Here, God's presence is known intuitively, and the soul becomes increasingly free to follow the leadings of the Spirit without being disturbed by attachments, addictions, and other worldly influences.

G. Thus it is that the soul is deified, or made able to know God as Christ knows God. This is the fruit of the spiritual journey, and the reason for which we were created.

15.

Charismatic Gifts

Every person has both natural gifts and spiritual gifts. Natural gifts refer to those aptitudes you have received from your parents; they are genetically based and include such gifts as verbal skills, mathematical ability, physical coordination and so forth. Author Howard Gardner's research on multiple intelligences is a good way to understand what we mean by natural gifts. We all have abilities in the seven areas of intelligence described by Gardner, but some people have higher potential in some areas than others. One's upbringing and commitment to practicing skills also determines how our natural gifts develop.

Spiritual gifts are of two kinds: those we give away (charismatic gifts) and those we give keep (transformative gifts). This chapter is about charismatic gifts; the next will be about the transformative gifts of the Spirit.

Charismatic gifts are given to us by the Holy Spirit for the good of the community. A traditional listing of these can be found in 1 Cor. 12:4-10; it is likely that there are many more, and theologians who have studied this topic have indeed expanded the listing. Unlike natural gifts, these do not "belong" to us; they are given by the Spirit when the need arises. Like natural gifts, however, we can grow in our familiarity with a spiritual gift and its application as we make use of it.

Discovering Your Spiritual Gifts

There are many wonderful web sites (some listed below) that provide spiritual gift inventories to enable a general understanding of your primary spiritual gifts. The web site at http://www.siena.org/ also has a wealth of information. The quote below from their web site summarizes the significance of these charisms in the spiritual life:

Discerning and exercising one's charisms can be a wonderful catalyst of spiritual growth.

> Few things nurture faith in God's loving presence like seeing God's provision and goodness reach others through the charisms of an ordinary person like you or me. The spiritual disciplines necessary to mature in the use of a charism change us and help transform us into more Christ-like people.

Understanding our charisms can free us from the need to compare ourselves with others and from judging others because they are different from us.

> Participants (in their workshops) regularly comment about how healing an experience it is to discern their gifts. Those who judged themselves for not measuring up to someone else's standard are freed by recognizing that their giftedness and calling may be different. Those who judged other Christians for having different priorities are able to relax and recognize the validity of the many calls within the larger Body of Christ.

Every charism represents a call from God. Becoming clear about the charisms that you have been given can greatly clarify decision-making.

> A lot of energy is released for service as individuals begin to acknowledge where they are not gifted and begin to concentrate on the areas where they are called and gifted.

Understanding your charisms helps prevent unnecessary failure and burn-out.

> Charisms of the Holy Spirit enable us to be exceptionally effective for the Kingdom of God. It is unusually energizing and fulfilling to exercise a charism and we are much less likely to burn out if working in the arena of our giftedness.

The discernment of charisms can help individuals understand and name what they are already experiencing.
    (See http://www.siena.org/FAQ-Article/spiritual-gifts.html Permission to quote granted.)

The siena.org web site lists three signs that indicate the presence of a charism.

1. When you exercise the charism, you feel energized, and a closeness to God.
2. Other people give you positive feedback concerning your exercising of this gift.
3. You are effective when you exercise the gift. E.g., healings happen when healers pray for people; teachers can convey knowledge, etc.

Keeping these three considerations in mind, what kinds of spiritual gifts do you think you've been blessed with?

Resources

There are a few web sites that provide inventories and even online questionnaires to help you begin to identify the charisms given to you. Some are more comprehensive than others, but give them all a try and see what you come up with.

- http://www.churchgrowth.org/cgi-cg/gifts.cgi
- http://www.cforc.com/sgifts.html
- http://buildingchurch.net/g2s.htm
- http://mintools.com/spiritual-gifts-test.htm

The topic of spiritual gifts is a good one to touch base on from time to time in spiritual direction.

16.

Transformative Gifts

In Isaiah 11:2-3, we read:

The Spirit of the LORD will rest on him —
the Spirit of wisdom and of understanding,
the Spirit of counsel and of power,
the Spirit of knowledge and of the fear of the Lord.
And he will delight in the fear of the Lord . . .

These describe the character of the Messiah to come. Later Christian tradition also came to understand them as gifts of the Spirit that transform human character, conforming it to that of Christ. As such, then, these seven, transformative gifts of the Spirit are ours to keep, although they certainly enrich our capacity to give as well. But they are not the same as the charismatic gifts mentioned in our previous chapter.

What follows is a short description of each of the gifts:

1. *Wisdom* enables us to recognize the workings of God in the world and in our lives. It transforms our intellectual capacity so we can make better judgments in conformity with truth and love.
2. *Understanding* helps us to sift out truth from falsehood, thus working in concert with the gift of wisdom.
3. *Counsel* pertains to the ethical life, helping us to choose the good and reject what is wrong.
4. *Power* (also called Courage or Fortitude) strengthens the will to overcome fear that we might stand up for what is right.
5. *Knowledge* enables us to understand the meaning of divine revelation.

6. *Fear of the Lord* gifts us with wonder and awe before God and creation, helping us to be humble and grateful.
7. *Piety* moves us to reverence and worship, giving praise and glory to God for the countless gifts bestowed upon us.

There is much more that could be written about each of these, and doing more research on the transformative gifts of the Spirit would be a good topic of study. After learning more about the gifts, you could then consider how, in your own life, you experience each of these at work in you, helping to transform your own character unto a likeness of Christ's. Also, consider the growth you have seen in each of these gifts through the years. Discussing all this with your spiritual director would be a beneficial exercise.

17.

Type and Temperament

There are a number of approaches to account for differences among people, and some of these can help you to understand yourself and how you relate to other people and creation, including how you make decisions and even which methods of prayer are likely to work for you. Space does not permit a comprehensive listing and description of these approaches, so I will mention only two of them, here. It is likely that your spiritual director can point you to resources for each.

Jung's Psychological Types

The 20th century psychiatrist, Carl Jung, wrote much about human differences. Terms we use today like "introvert" and "extravert" have come into popular use largely because of Jung's work. Basically, he looked at three different opposing tendencies in how our consciousness operates, and noted that each of us prefers one of these over the other.

A. Attitude

1. Introverts are more attuned to the inner world.
2. Extraverts are more attuned to the outer world.

B. Perception

1. Sensates notice details and tend to be very practical.
2. Intuitives notice possibilities and tend to be dreamers.

C. Judging

1. Thinkers make decisions using logic.
2. Feelers consider emotion and relationships in making decisions.

Jung's psychological types consider different combinations of these operations — for example: Introverted-Sensate-Feeling types.

Individuals of this type tend to see the world very differently than their opposite type: Extraverted-Intuitive-Thinkers.

There are a number of inventories that can help you to better understand your psychological type, the most popular being the Myers-Briggs-Type-Indicator (MBTI). Another is called the Kiersey-Bates Temperament Sorter. Do an Internet search for these and you will find free inventories online, along with helpful reading material.

Enneagram

The Enneagram is another popular approach to understanding human differences. Its development has gone through a number of phases, the most recent being in the 20th C. by G. I. Gurdjieff, Oscar Ichazo and Claudio Naranjo.

Basically, Enneagram theory proposes that we have three energy centers — head, heart and gut — and that we prefer operating out of one of these over the other two. Each of these three centers has three orientations: to the outer world, to the inner world, or a balance between. The result is nine Enneagram types, designated by numbers, each having distinctive virtues, vices and compulsive tendencies. A triangle superimposed on a circle is used to arrange the types, with the three balanced numbers — 3, 6, and 9 — on the points of the triangles.

As with Jung's psychological types, there are quite a few web sites and books on the Enneagram and these can help you to come to understand your own Enneagram type. If your spiritual director has received training with the Enneagram, he or she can help you to understand its relevance to living more fully. Many retreat centers offer workshops on the Enneagram as well, so check out what's available in your area.

18.

Spiritual Pathways

Every world religion recognizes that different individuals have different ways of traversing on the spiritual journey. No doubt this is related to psychological types (previous chapter) but there may be other factors at work as well, such as one's natural and spiritual giftedness.

Learning to identify your primary spiritual pathway can be helpful in many ways, as it's most likely that you will be happiest and find the closest possible relationship with God if you are true to yourself, here. Obviously, this topic is also a good one to discuss and discern in spiritual direction.

What follows are a few ways that different writers and spiritual traditions have described spiritual pathways. See which ones you identify with.

Christian Tradition

1. *Monastic* - highly structured communal life; contemplative focus; most introverted types would do well, here.
2. <u>*Contemplative/psychological*</u> - Dominicans, Carmelites, etc. Contemplative focus, but also somewhat active in the world. Action flowing from contemplation. Mostly introverted types.
3. *Apostolic* - Jesuits, Franciscans, Diocesan Priests, Protestantism, laity. Ideal for extraverted types.

Yogic pathways correlated with Jung's psychological types

1. *The Way of Loving Devotion.* Loving God with one's whole heart.
   a. Most natural for feeling types.
   b. Committed relationship with the Beloved. Recognizing the Beloved in all people and creation.
   c. Ethics implicit in the demands of relationship.
   d. Self-centeredness killed in love for the good of the Other.
   e. Examples: Biblical "Song of Songs." Devotional Christianity. Bhakti yoga.
2. *The Way of Service.* Loving God with one's whole strength.
   a. Most natural for all extraverted and sensate types.
   b. Selfless action for the glory of God.
   c. Ethics implicit in the demands of service and daily work.
   d. Self-centeredness killed in detachment from results of service.
   e. Examples: Mother Theresa. Jesuit/lay spirituality. Karma yoga.
3. *The Way of Knowledge.* Loving God with one's whole mind.
   a. Most natural for introverted thinking and introverted intuition types..
   b. Discovery of God as the Source of all Truth.
   c. Ethics implicit in the order of the universe.
   d. Self-centeredness killed by detachment, discrimination, and dis-identification with Egoic elements.
   e. Examples: St. Thomas Aquinas. Jnana yoga.
4. *The Way of Insight.* Loving God with one's whole soul.
   a. Most natural for introverted intuition types.
   b. Discovery of God as the Source of one's being. Intrapersonal exploration. Somewhat impersonal mysticism.
   c. Ethics implicit in the requirements of inner silence.

    d. Self-centeredness killed by absorption in deep Silence.

    e. Examples: Meister Eckhart. Anthony de Mello. Trappists. Raja yoga.

Four Pathways of Creation Spirituality (Matthew Fox)

1. The *Via Positiva* is about awe and wonder and the joy and praise that comes from truly beholding Nature and Creation.

2. The next path is the *Via Negativa:* the way of darkness, suffering, silence, letting go, and even nothingness.

3. In the *Via Creativa* we co-create with God; in our imaginative output, we trust our images enough to birth them into existence. This is Path Three.

4. The fourth path is the *Via Transformativa*, the transformative way. This is a path of compassion, the relief of suffering, the combating of injustice, of speaking up for those who have no voice.

19.

Stages of Spiritual Growth

What follows are several ways of charting the spiritual journey. Each has its own unique perspective; see if you can identify yourself in these descriptions, and, after a few sessions, discuss this with your spiritual director. See what determinations the two of you together come up with.

The web site url for each of these provides much more detailed information and description. Be sure to check it out.

M. Scott Peck's four stages:
(See http://www.escapefromwatchtower.com/stages.html)
1. *Chaotic, Antisocial.* These people are mostly self-centered. If they are involved in a religious tradition, it is mostly for show.
2. *Formal, Institutional, Fundamental.* Individuals in this stage attempt to live by laws or principles as they recognize the value of such, but they do not grasp yet the inner meaning of these principles. Theirs is more an external conformity, even though sincerely lived out.
3. *Skeptic, Individual, Questioner.* Can include atheists, agnostics and believers. These people sincerely question their beliefs and the reasons for their beliefs. They choose to live by principles that make sense to them.
4. *Mystic, Communal.* Individuals motivated to live by love for the good of all (including the planet), not merely oneself or one's family or country. They are generally part of a religious tradition, but not always.

James Fowler: Stages of Faith Development

http://faculty.plts.edu/gpence/html/fowler.htm)

1. *Intuitive-Projective* faith is the fantasy-filled, imitative phase in which the child can be powerfully and permanently influenced by examples, moods, actions and stories of the visible faith of primally related adults. . .

2. *Mythic-Literal* faith is the stage in which the person begins to take on for him- or herself the stories, beliefs and observances that symbolize belonging to his or her community. . .

3. *Synthetic-Conventional* faith, a person's experience of the world now extends beyond the family. A number of spheres demand attention: family, school or work, peers, street society and media, and perhaps religion. . .

4. *Individuative-Reflective* faith is particularly critical for it is in this transition that the late adolescent or adult must begin to take seriously the burden of responsibility for his or her own commitments, lifestyle, beliefs and attitudes. . .

5. *Conjunctive* faith involves the integration into self and outlook of much that was suppressed or unrecognized in the interest of Stage 4's self-certainty and conscious cognitive and affective adaptation to reality. . .

6. *Universalist.* The persons best described by it have generated faith compositions in which their felt sense of an ultimate environment is inclusive of all being. They have become incarnators and actualizers of the spirit of an inclusive and fulfilled human community.

Teresa of Avila's Seven Mansions

http://www.ourgardenofcarmel.org/castle.html

1. The souls in the *First Mansions* are drawn by God's grace, but are still attracted to the "old life" they've left behind, to which they occasionally return.
2. The *Second Mansions* mark a turning point of commitment to spiritual growth. Here one begins to read more, pray more, and practice virtue more conscientiously.
3. The *Third Mansions* indicate the development of habitual virtue and consistent commitment to spiritual practice. One's identity has shifted so that worldly things are no longer attractive.
4. In the *Fourth Mansion*, there is greater ease in living the spiritual life as one has become more acclimated to God's grace, which supplies for every need. It is also, for some, the beginnings of mystical prayer.
5. For those called to mystical prayer, the *Fifth Mansion* brings a deepening of such prayer, often with many mystical experiences.
6. St. Teresa called the *Sixth Mansion* the time of betrothal to the beloved. It is also a time for deepening mystical prayer.
7. The *Seventh Mansion* brings mystical marriage and the fullest possible union between and individual and God to be known in this world.

Classical Christian Stages

(See http://www.newadvent.org/cathen/14254a.htm - public domain.)

1. The *purgative way* is the way, or state, of those who are beginners, that is, those who have obtained justification, but have not their passions and evil inclinations in such a state of subjugation that they can easily overcome temptations, and who, in order to preserve and exercise charity and the other virtues have to keep up a continual warfare within themselves. . .

2. The *illuminative way* is that of those who are in the state of progress and have their passions better under control, so that they easily keep themselves from serious wrongdoing, but who do not so easily avoid minor sins, because they still take pleasure in earthly things and allow their minds to be distracted by various imaginations and their hearts with numberless desires, though not in matters that are strictly unlawful. It is called the illuminative way, because in it the mind becomes more and more enlightened as to spiritual things and the practice of virtue. . .

3. The *unitive way* is the way of those who are in the state of the perfect, that is, those who have their minds so drawn away from all temporal things that they enjoy great peace, who are neither agitated by various desires nor moved by any great extent by passion, and who have their minds chiefly fixed on God and their attention turned, either always or very frequently, to Him. It is the union with God by love and the actual experience and exercise of that love. . .

20.

Writing Your Mission Statement

A mission statement is a short summary of "what you want to be and do—what qualities you want to develop, what you want to accomplish, what contributions you want to make." (Steven Covey). Writing a mission statement in spiritual direction can be an excellent process for discerning God's call into the future.

In the life of Christian faith, there are a few spiritual principles that can help to inform your mission statement:

1. God has created you a good and unique human being.
2. God's unconditional love desires your growth and happiness.
3. It is God's will that you become the unique person whom God has created you to be.
4. Cherishing and developing your uniqueness is consistent with "doing God's will."
5. Your happiness gives glory to God.

Do these principles describe something of your understanding of God and God's will?

Guiding Questions
1. What do you perceive to be your strongest gifts?
2. What values are most important to you?
3. What do you enjoy doing most?
4. If you could do anything you wanted and resources were no problem, what would you do? Where and how would you live?
5. What relationships are most important to you? What do you hope to be able to say about these relationships in five years?

6. What kind of epitaph would you like to have written on your tomb?

Writing the Statement

After spending time reflecting and journaling with the above questions, jot down a few phrases that summarize your core beliefs about who you are and what you are to be about in your life. Write it in the first person ("I, Jane Doe, affirm. . .") or as a prayer. Let your first draft come spontaneously. . . don't worry about grammar, punctuation, redundancy.

Once you're in touch with the core principles and affirmations that comprise your mission, compose the final draft of your statement. Try to keep it short — no more than two or three sentences. When done, post it someplace where you can review it frequently (journal, calendar, prayer book, framed on a wall). Use it as a meditation, an examination of consciousness, an energizing source of affirmation and direction for you. Bring a copy to your spiritual director and discuss what this process was like for you.

21.

Writing Your Own Rule (or Way) of Life

A Rule of Life is most associated with Catholic religious orders, who use the Rule to outline what is important to deepen the development and expression of their spirituality and to honor their distinctive spiritual gifts. If you have come to a better sense of your own gifts and have done the mission statement exercise that preceded this one, you are ready to write your own Rule of Life.

First a word about the term, "Rule," however. For many, this connotes images of all sorts of "do's" and "don'ts." Understandably so, for that is the usual meaning of the term. In the context used in spirituality, however, it identifies essential practices for growing on the spiritual journey. The "Rule," then, might be understood as a kind of covenant you make with God—a way of saying that you intend to do what is necessary to grow as fully as God is calling you to grow.

Let's get started . . .

A. *Begin by reviewing your Mission Statement.* Keep this vision in mind throughout the process. You might even consider using your Mission Statement as the opening paragraph for your Rule of Life.

B. *Growing in Relationships*
  1. With God. What practices do you need to do to remain close to God? Be specific here, including how much time to give to them, when, how often, etc. One suggestion, here, is to make a list of practices for daily, weekly, monthly and yearly attention. Next to each of the practices listed above, indicate its importance to you using a rating scale of 1-5.
  Under the heading of "Growing in Relationship with God," write out what you commit yourself to doing daily, weekly, monthly

and yearly. Be specific in describing the practice for each time period.

2. With Family. You can repeat the 3 steps listed above for other relationships — e.g., marriage, children, friends, and so forth. In spiritual direction, we are most concerned with developing your relationship with God, but the others are obviously relevant, as are the following points, which you might also wish to pursue at some time.

C. *Caring for Self*

1. What practices do you need to do to properly care for your body? Follow the process steps in B1 above to come to your decision and write your response.

2. What practices do you need to do to properly care for your psyche (mind, emotions, imagination, memories)? Again, follow the Steps in B1. Be sure to consider factors like fun, play and so forth.

3. Any other aspect of caring for self you want to consider, repeating the process steps of B1.

D. *Service and Work*

1. Make a list of specific ways you can give witness to your faith and values in the work place and everyday life. Brainstorm specific behaviors and practices. Rate each of these behaviors on a scale of 1-5.

2. For behaviors and practices you value highly, write out what you would like to commit yourself to do, when, etc.

3. Make a list of specific ways you can give witness to your faith in your faith community. Repeat the Steps of D1 and D2.

E. *Overall Lifestyle*

1. What kind of lifestyle seems most consonant with the values you have identified above? Consider the following:
   a. Urban vs. suburban vs. rural
   b. Wealthy vs. middle income vs. poverty
   c. Married, single, religious life.
   d. Conventional vs. alternative / simple
      And so forth . . .
2. What values do you wish to commit yourself to expressing in your overall lifestyle? Consider your reflections from E1 and any others you might wish to identify.
3. Write a statement listing the values from E 2 and how you would like to give evidence of these in your lifestyle.

F. Bringing it all together.

Now it is time to write your Rule of Life. One possibility is to begin with your Mission Statement, then to organize your Rule using the five areas listed above. For each, write a short statement summarizing your principles and beliefs, then follow with a listing of specific behaviors and practices you will commit to doing to give evidence of these beliefs. Be specific, here; the behaviors should be measurable. E.g., "I commit myself to at least 20 min. of prayer every day" rather than "to pray regularly."

Throughout this process, let your spiritual director know how it's going, and request feedback.

A Few Recommended Resources

Books

Bakke, Jeanette. *Holy Listening: Exploring Spiritual Direction.* Baker Books. 2000.

Barry, William A. and William J. Connolly. *The Practice of Spiritual Direction.* Harper One. 2009.

Dubay, Thomas. *Seeking Spiritual Direction: How to Grow the Divine Life Within.* Servant Publ. 1994.

Green, Thomas H., S.J. *The Friend of the Bridegroom: Spiritual Direction and the Encounter With Christ.* Ave Maria Press. 1999.

May, Gerald G. *Care of Mind, Care of Spirit.* Harper One. 1992.

Peterson, Eugene H. *The Contemplative Pastor: Returning to the Art of Spiritual Direction.* W. B. Eerdmans. 1993.

Web Sites

Heartland Center for Spirituality
  www.heartlandspirituality.org

Shalom Place
  www.shalomplace.com

Spiritual Directors International
  www.sdiworld.org

Wikipedia on "Spiritual Direction"
  http://en.wikipedia.org/wiki/Spiritual_direction